Living   Creating   Collecting

Blue and White Japan

Blue and White Japan

Amy Sylvester Katoh

Photographs by Yutaka Satoh

TUTTLE PUBLISHING
Boston • Rutland, Vermont • Tokyo

For Yuichi, the sun, Mia, Saya, Tai, and Toshi, the stars, Okasama and Obachama, sister moons,
and Edmund Quincy Sylvester, who filled the skies with kites and rockets

No book is written alone. This one is the sum of generous servings of help and cooperation from friends and people we admire who shared their blue and white rooms and collections and recipes without stint. To Sanshiro Ikeda for his blessings, Seiji and Harumi Nibe for creative guidance, Bill and Angela Cruger, Martyne and Tom Kupciunas, Hiroshi and Noriyuki Murata of Kosoen, Chie and Hideki Maegawa, Haruri Ginka Gallery, Mr. and Mrs. Susumu Kakitani, Betty and Gil Hoffman for their consummate hospitality, Henk and Alison Hoksbergen, Tamiko and Tsutomu Makishi, Yasuko and Jissei Omine, Mrs. Yoshiko Shimabukuro of the Daiichi Hotel, Naha, Okinawa, the Matsuda brothers of the Yomitan potters' guild, Sachiko Kinjo, the Kumamoto family of Pension Bisezaki, Katsuko and Shungo Shoji, Hiroyuki Shindo for his indigo inspiration, Kenji and Aiko Tanaka, Yoshihiro Takishita of the House of Antiques for his expertise, Kazuko and Tadashi Morita of Morita Antiques for their knowledge, Yoshichika Kitamura, Chikako and Masanobu Matsumoto of the Gifu Bamboo Society, Shokichi Watanabe and Setsuko Shinoda of Gujo Hachiman, Kibo and Keiko Nomoto, Michiko Natsuhara, Noriko Mikawa, Andrea Heinrichsohn, Kim Schuefftan for his knowledge, Koichi Hama for his calligraphy, Takako Fukuchi and Takako Enokido for their dedication, Hiroko Izumi, Mitsu Minowa for her cooking, Kyoko Machida, Kazuko Yoshiura for her *sashiko*, Reiko Okunushi for her quilts, Paula Deitz for her ikat skies. To you all, and unnamed others, thank you.

Inside covers: *Three hundred and fifty years of Imari. Seventeenth-through-twentieth-century soba cups, from the collection of Susumu Kakitani.*
Page 2: *Blue and white welcome. Umbrella stand and old wooden planting frame covered with paper handmade by Kiyomi Tomi of Wajima and painted by Takako Fukuchi. A vintage bedcover of patches over patches is the welcome mat.*
Above: *Imari dish in the shape of Otafuku, a jolly household goddess.*
Right: *Carp and waterfall design with bubbles on a fragment of an old hemp futon cover.*
Page 81: *Photo courtesy of La Seine magazine.*

Published by Tuttle Publishing,
an imprint of Periplus Editions (HK) Ltd.

LCC Card No. 95-62393
ISBN 0-8048-3305-2

First paperback edition, 2002
Second printing, 2002

Printed in Singapore

Contents

Introduction

Japan speaks in blue and white. Azure waves wash over worn Imari shards half-buried in white sand; cotton-ball clouds drift across cobalt skies. Indigo doorway curtains distinguish shop fronts in small mountain towns; old ladies on their way to the neighborhood bath shuffle by in blue and white robes. An unknown dyer has captured the magic of cranes on a graceful padded indigo sleeping kimono. "Mountain flowers like white brocade, valley water brimming indigo," wrote the poet Issa in the eighteenth century. This felicitous marriage of color is loved the world round, but its transcendent expression is found in Japan, where nature's prototype has long inspired artists and craftsmen to apply blue and white to cloth and clay, picture and poem.

Blue and white porcelains and textiles in particular have played an integral part in the history of Japan and figure prominently in myth and literature. From the blue and white streamers that helped lure the Sun Goddess Amaterasu out of the cave where she hid in anger at her brother, plunging the world into darkness, to the bolts of blue and white silk given in tribute to Chinese emperors centuries ago, to the

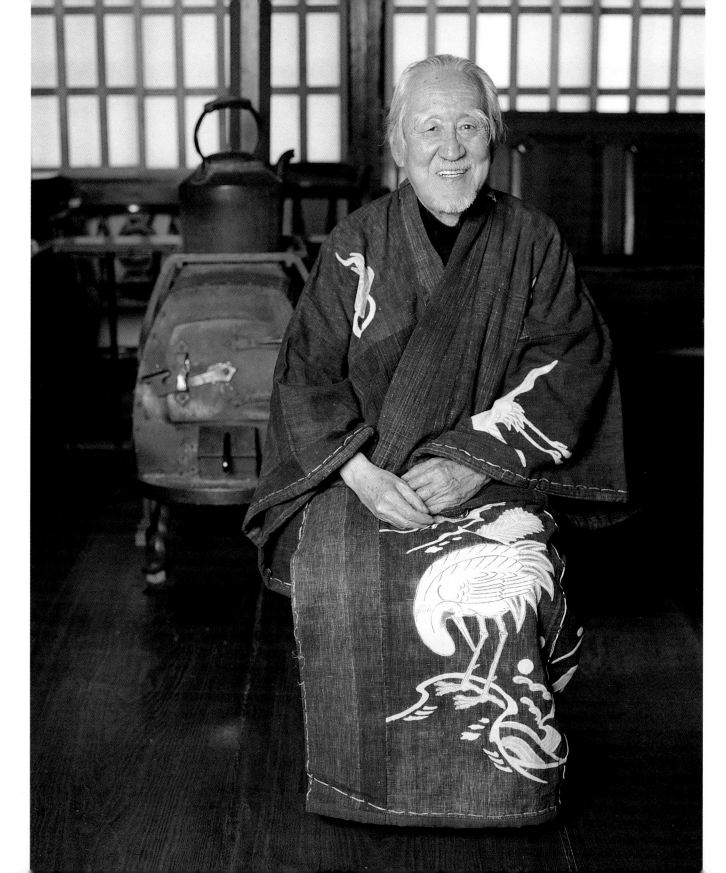

blue and white Imari porcelains that were staples in the Dutch East India Company's trade with Europe, blue and white have long been the colors Japan has made its name with throughout the world. Today, new combinations and arrangements are constantly being created, but the essential impact of this basic color combination remains as fresh and powerful as it first was thousands of years ago.

The objective reasons for my love of blue and white are easier to explain than the subjective ones. When I first arrived in Japan, fresh out of college, I was struck by the constant presence of these colors. The blue and white aesthetic was one I had grown up with in Massachusetts, and it made me feel instantly at home when I found it repeated everywhere in Japan. Craftsmen responded to the natural world around them with blue and white creations in textiles and ceramics. From *futon* quilts and cotton kimono, to bowls and plates and porcelains of all kinds, many of the things I used each day were blue and white. Blue and white seemed to surround me and invite me to stay. But it wasn't just an aesthetic attraction. Most appealing was the fact that blue and white was the basic color combination of ordinary life. Not of fancy, sophisticated Japan, but of down-to-earth Japan. It was the *tenugui* hand towel. It was the last thing worn at night, the crisp, comforting *yukata* robe slipped on after the bath. Blue and white recurred at every level of daily human activity. Craftsmen pulled on indigo workclothes to perform their labor. Men and women in the fields wore baggy indigo trousers and short wrapped jackets. Workmen tied cotton hand towels dyed in simple blue stenciled designs around their heads or tucked them into their belts. Although a haughty, aristocratic blue and white was visible in the most precious porcelain platters and bowls, the blue and white that caught my twenty-year-old eye was the homely blue and white of everyday Japan. The no-big-deal teapots hanging from nails in the rafters of neighborhood crockery shops. The plates and cups of every shape and size that overflowed a table to serve even a simple breakfast. Blue and white dishes were so commonplace, no one thought twice about the luxury of using them unsparingly, though I used to despair when it was my turn to wash.

Handmade crafts were one of the few things old, frugal Japan had in profusion. Human effort and unmatched craftsmanship compensated for a lack of resources and natural bounty. With dextrous hands, craftsmen produced dishes and cloth for daily living that they colored blue and white. From about the sixth century in Japan, indigo was domesticated and used to dye cloth. Cobalt underglaze-

decorated porcelain was already well developed by 1700. Artisans used blue against the absence of blue (white) to create basic patterns, distillations of larger motifs in nature that were masterpieces of design. When I came to Japan thirty years ago, it was another time, another country. Today's high-tech, fast-paced society ignores old traditions. The knowledge of how to create some of the intricate patterns found in antique textiles is being lost. The soft colors on porcelain bowls of long ago are rarely found on new pieces sold in department stores. The blues are harsher now, the whites too white. Many of the craftsmen I used to visit are gone, and their sons do not want to learn the old techniques. And yet — the economic doldrums of the 1990s may provide a way for Japan to find itself again. As the country comes to terms with the limitations of growth, it is beginning to reconsider and rediscover what is real, what is precious, and what is quintessentially Japanese. To me, blue and white is Japan. Though these colors occur elsewhere, the Japanese response to blue and white is original and inspired. It pervades crafts and arts and daily life in a way that is found in no other country. As such, blue and white Japan is worth searching out and celebrating. Most of all, it is worth trying to capture its magic in our houses and living spaces today.

Living with blue and white

means the focus is on simplicity. Here, peace prevails in the entrance-way of the Sanshiro Ikeda house, moved from Toyama Prefecture twenty-five years ago and faithfully restored in Matsumoto. The lines of the alternating slats of dark wood on the sliding door are repeated in the bamboo pattern of the hemp-fiber *noren* curtain created by the late Keisuke Serizawa, stencil designer, dyer, and Living National Treasure. On the massive chest are an old quilt and a *furoshiki,* wrapping cloth.

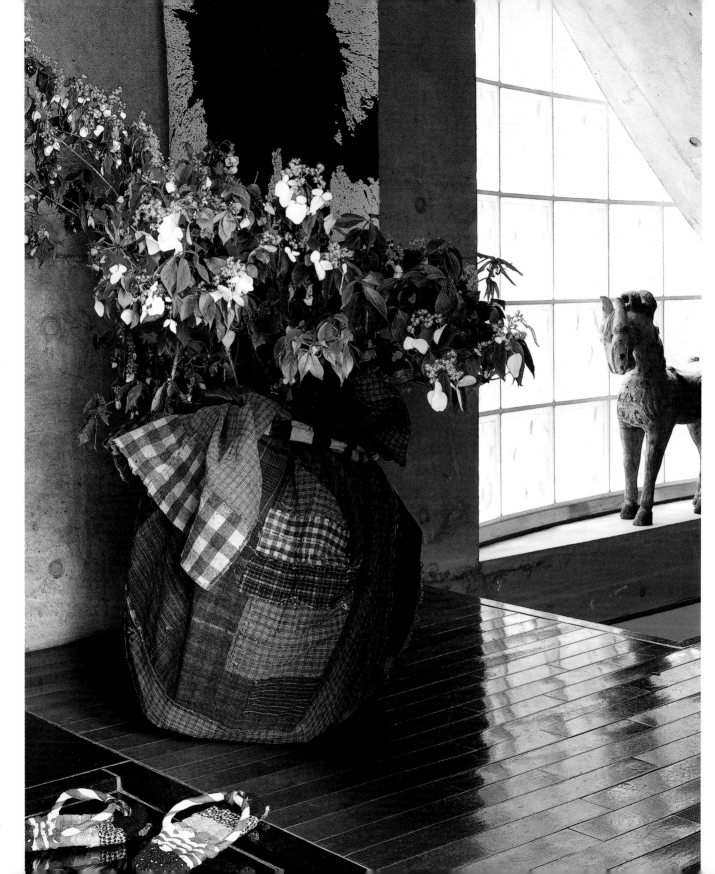

Entrances

Entrances not only welcome visitors, they also reflect the taste of those who live within. They are considered the face of the home. What better place to introduce a blue and white sensibility? Blue and white has its own energy and it conveys a message of simplicity and order. Start with basic materials — an Imari umbrella stand, a favorite porcelain *hibachi* brazier, some antique textiles — then use them in fresh ways to add texture and character to otherwise anonymous spaces. Try wrapping a basket of flowers and branches in an old *futon* cover of patched indigo. Add a touch of whimsy to an entranceway floor with an arrangement of ragweave sandals and heavy workman's footwear. Consider using *noren,* the split curtains traditionally hung in shop doorways, to delineate space and serve as creative door dressing. Then, in the Japanese way, change them with the seasons: sheer fabrics for summer, thick cotton indigo in cold weather. The entrance is a place to make a statement about what you love and what gives you energy. Share that energy with all who enter by making it an expression of your individuality. Blue and white is the message. The entrance is the place to communicate it.

Left: Rags and riches fill the entrance of the Kupciunas house. Calligraphy on a scroll of *washi,* Japanese handmade paper, by Naoaki Sakamoto of Paper Nao. The ragweave slippers are from Wajima. A Thai horse looks on.
Below: Wooden puppet's feet, workman's footwear, and old ragweave sandals join forces.

Left: A floor-to-ceiling indigo bamboo grove with openings cut for arrangements of hydrangeas in front of a sculpted concrete staircase and a child's kimono.
Below: Harumi Nibe, in a tie-dyed indigo hat by Ryoko Kodama, greets guests with her Labrador, Tokiwa Gozen. Next to her, a blue and white hemp curtain fragment draped over a freshly cut bamboo lintel serves as a new take on traditional *noren.* Transplanted to Tokyo from Shikoku, Nibe-san is a flower and food artist who brings the rich flavor of country sensibilities to whatever she does. Her style is imbued with the Japanese appreciation for rustic and natural things.

Above: Gossamer *noren* cover a storage cupboard in the display room of Kosoen, an indigo dyer's workshop in Ome, Tokyo. Above the cupboard, a rice-straw bale of fermented indigo sits next to rolls and skeins of undyed cotton thread. On the floor, an old back basket filled with lilies. In the next room are the indigo vats.

Right: A converted temple in Sakakitamura, Nagano, is home, workplace, and showroom for Kibo and Keiko Nomoto, potter/indigo dyer and textile artist respectively. Provisions for going out include an indigo traveling coat, paper umbrella, and covered clogs. Keiko Nomoto's own indigo patchwork collage brightens the wall.

Artful doors. Handsome

definers of space that invite us to enter a house or a room, *noren* can also turn a doorway into a frame for a fluid work of textile art.

Noren are usually dyed with indigo and made of cotton, and sometimes of hemp. They are suspended from a bamboo pole across the front of traditional Japanese shops, where they serve to announce both the name and crest/symbol of an establishment and that it is open for business. When the shop is closed, the *noren* is removed.

In the eighteenth and nineteenth centuries, streets were lined with shops whose vibrant *noren* were a compelling testament to the dyer's art. While modern stores do not usually hang *noren* above their entrances, enough *noren*-graced doorways still exist to offer practical art opportunities to indigo dyers and designers who seek a canvas on which to exhibit their talents.

Above: *Noren* in banana fiber and indigo, spun, woven, and dyed by Toshiko Taira of Okinawa, who has led the movement to preserve the ancient craft of banana-fiber textiles, *bashofu*.
Right: Tie-dyed indigo *noren* hanging in the doorway of the Kakinoki antique shop in Tokorozawa.
Facing page: Sheer magic. An appliquéd *noren* of indigo mosquito netting by Kazuko Yoshiura.

The best rooms

have a certain serenity and clarity of purpose. To the Japanese way of thinking, a main room where guests may visit has to be versatile and beautiful. It should also provide a feeling of well-being. Translated into a Western setting, this means the sort of uncluttered living room where you can put your feet up if you feel like it, throw a party when the spirit moves you, or just sit quietly by the window and daydream, yet always feel refreshed and sustained by things you love. Nestled on a hill in Okinawa overlooking the East China Sea, the room at left meets all these criteria. It is a living room where one is meant to live simply and well. The ever-changing blue and white of sea and sky are an evolving mural, so furniture and other decorative elements have been reduced and downplayed. Instead, the soaring windows provide a spirited sense of place through the use of local craftsmanship in the construction and the addition of blue and white Okinawan textiles and ceramic accents. Used in tandem with other things, blue and white lends a room a relaxed elegance, making it a room to remember.

Left: Straw cushions on the bay-window seat are favorite spots for tea. *Shisa,* temple dogs or lions, by Joga Shima, and a large blue and white covered bowl by Kyoshi Matsuda are dwarfed by the massive wall of local travertine in the fireplace.
Below: A pile of antique textiles waiting to be used.

Left: Country blues and whites in a mountain house in Kobuchizawa. Stretched along the sofa back is a 19th-century horse trapping. Quilted pillows in homespun cotton by Kazuko Yoshiura add comfort. An old, checkered fighting-dog blanket from Shikoku is under the table. Dogfights are now outlawed.

Above: Mood indigo in Haruri Ginka Gallery in Kawagoe. Under beams hung with dyed mosquito netting, a mysterious wooden llama sculpture by Hideki Maegawa shoulders an old *yukata* robe made of patched *tenugui* hand towels, while overseeing other whimsical Maegawa creations: tables and benches of old ships' timbers and other found objects, which he uses to create original furniture for living and laughing.

Above: A quirky sculpture by Seiji Nibe and a banner with a design of carp climbing a waterfall, a traditional symbol of strength and bravery, add panache to the entranceway of an apartment.

Right: A living room that welcomes friends to sit down, relax, and share stories among the owners' favorite things — books, family photos, rustic New England footstools, and, of course, blue and white pillows and floor cushions. The lamp on the right is by Isamu Noguchi. An indigo patchwork quilt does double duty as a rug, and a large lacquered tub, bought at a flea market years ago, serves as a coffee table.

Blue and white details

Simple things well arranged offer quiet inspiration. It is on details that the eye lingers — the enigmatic blue of a long striped textile against a sand-colored wall, the velvety white of a flower in a small Imari vase, the contrast of a checkered textile against richly worn wood. There is no substitute for attention to details in the creation of understated, relaxed style. Using blue and white ceramics that are more lovely than priceless, textiles that have individuality and charm above pedigree, adds intriguing character to a house. For fine-art devotees, imperfection is a flaw, but for those who love Japanese blue and white, a neatly mended antique cloth and a chipped plate carefully repaired and handed down through generations have stories to tell. They are intriguing because their lumps and bumps and mends reveal they are truly valued and cherished. Living with such objects is a joy. A tray of mismatched sake cups, a collection of porcelain shards, a favorite basket of fabric bits and pieces — all of these will brighten a room and evoke a warm response. A Japanese blue and white textile or ceramic has its own integrity, yet it interacts harmoniously with other objects and gives nourishment to all.

Left: 18th-century Japan in the 20th-century folk-art museum house of Sanshiro Ikeda, collector of furniture and crafts from Japan, England, and Korea. Here, a child's oak school desk and chair, an Imari vase, and a striped indigo textile with a family crest form a serene still life.
Below: A contemporary bamboo basket from Shiga Prefecture filled with blue and white ceramic scroll ends.

Floor cushions

No house in Japan should be without *zabuton,* versatile floor cushions that can create an instant seating area and then be stacked away once guests depart. *Zabuton* are traditionally filled with kapok or cotton padding.

Above: *Zabuton* covered in blue and white *kasuri,* ikat or patterned cotton, and modern textile adaptions of old indigo designs in between.

Left: Calligraphy practice on an antique glass-covered basket among scattered *zabuton* covered in vintage *kasuri* patterns. A ragweave farmer's vest in blue and white with red accents waits to be slipped on as the afternoon grows cooler. On the table, the dish and brush holder are old Imari, while the teapot and cup are contemporary.

Above: A giant red carp splashes up from a colorful textile on the sofa in the Hoksbergen living room. In front, a clever table constructed of lunch delivery boxes and glass. Below, a clouds-and-waves porcelain hibachi features a playful dragon.

Right: Something old, something new around the *irori,* a sunken open hearth, in a Yamanashi country house. The splendid heart-stopping cushions of indigo crosses on white hemp are by Takumi Sugawara, perhaps the most original *tsutsugaki,* freehand design, textile artist working today.

All in the details.

Japan, blue and white and otherwise, is an aggregate of details. Fine lines in small places, moods, moments. Focus with a Western eye on the grand picture and you may miss the quiet corners where the Japanese eye for particulars shines through. Look at the unheralded surfaces: the plasterer's roof gable, the tatami edging, the electrical outlet, the brush stroke on a piece of porcelain, the worn grain of a wooden tray. Peek at the under-kimono if you can. That is where the spirit is revealed.

Above: Handmade blue and white rope in an open-weave basket.

Left, from top: Maple leaves on an Imari plate; sake pourers and cups on an old wooden tray; porcelain umbrella stand with design of banana leaves; flowers, textiles, and odds and ends of porcelain waiting to be arranged for a shoot.

Facing page, clockwise from top: Waves and carp plaster design by Hitoshi Kutsukaki on a roof gable in a Karuizawa house; stone gods on ragweave *obi* sash; a striped horse rein used as edging for tatami; Meiji-era (1868–1912) glass lamp shade and Imari electrical fixture at Kakinoki Antique Gallery.

Facing page, above: Handmade chair belonging to Kibo Nomoto; 18th-century Windsor chair in the Sanshiro Ikeda collection with a checkerboard kimono; Charles Rennie Mackintosh chair with a tie-dyed indigo wool scarf by Ryoko Kodama.

Facing page, below: Chairmanship by Okinawan furniture maker Mitsuo Shiroma. A chair can be a hat rest or reading roost. Next to the chair, a pot by Jissei Omine holds a large banana leaf.

Left: A 19th-century Spanish daybed cushioned in blue and white tie-dyed material.

Below: Hideki and Chie Maegawa relax on an old Hokkaido horse sledge covered in stenciled *futon* material.

A fair chair. A good chair is an old
friend you can spend your life with. Covered in a treasured blue and white textile, even the most mundane bench can become a magical place to sit and dream, an individual, one-of-a-kind conversation piece and comfort center. Patches welcome! Past-their-prime textiles and fragments find a good home in chair cushions.

Confessions of a collector

I am a hoarder, an amasser, an accumulator of things. One thing brought home and found to bring pleasure inspires the search for another. Things multiply, pile up. A collection is born. Some fine collections begin in such snowflake fashion, but so do some irredeemable junk piles. The line between the two is fine.

For me, collecting begins at the flea market, where the energies and passions of other collectors and dealers rub together and create sparks. Initially, I was drawn to the muted blues and grayish whites of old Imari ceramics. The addiction to everything blue and white developed later. I found myself gravitating from noodle cups to incense dishes, from sake-cup stands to tiles and medicine bottles. Textiles were an obvious next step. First, blue and white stenciled cotton with attention-grabbing designs caught my eye. Then, I turned to quieter, more reticent pieces — hardworking tie-dyed farm clothes, ragweaves. Muted, worn, and often shabby, they nevertheless have a subtle beauty that holds its own against shiny Imari or assertive stenciled textiles. In the end, it is the quiet pieces that one wants to live with.

Gradually this collector's eye has turned away from what first

Right: An old striped horse trapping on the stairs at the Kupciunas house is a stage for a collection of patched indigo drawstring bags once used for carrying treasures from rice to coins in country Japan.
Below: A tattered drawstring bag holds its own in a modern setting.

attracted. I spent a luxurious day in Kyoto recently looking for textiles, something I hadn't done for a long time. I visited old friends, a few of Kyoto's textile dealers. Among their fine pieces, nothing really had the spark I was looking for. I went to the pre-auction exhibition of the semi-annual textile sales and poured over my choices from the catalogue. An amusing indigo elephant, quiet soft colors, outlandish proportions and details done by a textile artist who had surely never seen an

Right: Rabbits rampant. Wood, porcelain, clay, and bronze rabbits, gathered on an old storehouse door, impress by numbers, as well as by variety of medium and design.

elephant. A quilted farm jacket of intricate patterns, with a bonus pair of frolicking horses at the hem — the height of the stitcher's art. A patchwork *obi* sash of seventeenth-century cottons tenaciously stitched together, a demonstration of the frugality of the maker, the preciousness of each fragment, and the artfulness of design born of necessity. These were marvelous pieces, and I was glad to savor them with my eyes, but I felt no need to own them.

Just before boarding the train home I visited one last antique dealer and went through his stacks of indigo textiles. There were horse trappings and padded cotton kimono with auspicious designs hand-painted on the back. There were *tsutsugaki* towels and old quilts and back straps for carrying children. I enjoyed viewing this array of indigo art. But my heart did not stop until I found a forgotten fragment at the bottom of a pile. A bit of cloth with a brush-stroked bird sitting on a lotus seed pod captured a moment in sure white strokes on rough homespun cotton dyed a deep indigo and mended time after time by someone before me who treasured this magic blue and white fragment as I will.

Above: Lotus flower and pod with bird, a segment of a banner fragment, probably 19th century.
Right: Blue and white *tsutsugaki* pillows and a vintage coverlet of patched stenciled indigo on a chair made for reading and dreaming.

Right: A calligrapher's collection of brushes hung on a miniature stand is used by Alison Hoksbergen for her ink painting. An Imari teapot and other treasures are stored in the small *tansu* chest.

Below: A trio of antique blue and white *hibachi* used for growing water lilies in the garden.

Porcelain *hibachi,* traditional Japanese

charcoal braziers used for warming hands and rooms, are not easy to collect these days, as good ones are becoming scarce. But fine examples occasionally can be found in antique shops and at flea markets. *Hibachi* were once a luxury item for the upper classes, but as charcoal became readily available in the seventeenth century, wooden *hibachi* with copper liners appeared in ordinary households. When Japan's porcelain industry expanded during the Meiji Restoration, porcelain *hibachi* became popular, especially those hand-painted by Kyushu craftsmen in blue and white patterns.

Later, stencil techniques were used to speed up production and meet growing consumer demand. *Hibachi* are both charming and practical, whether used as intended as braziers or given a new lease on life as flowerpots, table supports, or homes for goldfish.

Above: International bottle convention on the window sill of Harumi Nibe's kitchen. Italian, French, and Japanese bottles, blue and otherwise, create a translucent sparkling tableau.

Right: A collection of blue and white water droppers nestles on an Okinawan silk scarf spun and hand-woven by Tamiko Makishi.

Left: Spiral designs on a collection of sake cups and pourers call for another round!
Below: Blue and white *soba*-noodle cups and flowers in the drawers of an old medicine chest at the Hoksbergen residence. On top, Imari vases stand in front of a proverb painting by Koji Ikeda.

Bedside manners.

As any designing woman or man will tell you, there is no reason not to have fun in the bedroom. Owning a blue and white textile or ceramic is not enough. To experience the true joy of your find, the new piece must have its place in your interior life. Adding well-loved textiles or ceramics to bedrooms brings personal style and taste into private havens. Family mementos, field grasses bursting from a *hibachi,* photos and books, all create an atmosphere of well-being. A much-loved antique quilt is a dear friend and a joy to wake up with each morning. Blue and white cushions add spice to sleeping quarters. A four-poster bed swathed in *yukata* fabric can become a one-of-a-kind place to dream. Old textiles found at flea markets are often fragments with tears and parts missing. They find new life when recycled as unique and spunky pillows, or patched or woven together into an unusual rug. Larger pieces — a still-intact *futon* cover, a giant indigo *tsutsugaki* square — work beautifully as bedcovers. Try combining Western bedding with Japanese blue and white textiles to create bedrooms that express remarkable individuality and help dreamers to wake up inspired.

Left: A tatami-mat sleeping platform is a private island of tranquility and peace. Surrounded by favorite things, from books to family photos to a crane-motif *hibachi,* and under a large blue and white arabesque-pattern duvet cover, you are invited to dream.
Below: A stack of rectangular cushions covered in *kasuri-*patterned indigo.

Below: The scarecrow by Takako Fukuchi and Takako Enomoto of Blue and White, which won first prize in the East Azabu neighborhood scarecrow competition, wears a blue and white *yukata*. On the daybed, a vibrant appliqué quilt by Reiko Okunushi displays a sampling of patterns found in *yukata* robes. Nearby, a tea box covered with *yukata* fabric is both end table and storage space.

Right: An appliqué quilt of indigo and other colored antique fabrics by Reiko Okunushi adds panache to the guest room of a Tokyo house. The quilt's motif is Otafuku, a jolly goddess of hearth and home. On the side table, a 19th-century bubble-patterned textile exudes faded charm.

Yukata

Yukata are light robes of breezy blue and white designs that have been stenciled onto narrow widths of cotton and then sewn into kimono shapes. Traditionally they were worn as robes after the bath to absorb moisture, but today that use survives mainly at hot-spring resorts. Most Japanese now wear *yukata* as summer kimono that are cool and comfortable. Not only the lightness and breathability of the cotton, but the psychological refreshment of the blue and white combination makes the wearer feel cool, even though the garment is long and full-sleeved.

Even today, Tokyo is the center of *yukata* production, inspiring hundreds of new patterns each year with its smart sense of style. (New patterns usually appear in department stores as summer draws near, but Blue and White in Azabu Juban features *yukata* fabrics in the latest designs year-round.) Patterns were originally drawn from sources in nature: birds, flowers, trees, animals, landscapes. A study of the history of *yukata* patterns is a study of Japanese graphic design in all its glory: strong, bracing reductions of natural phenomena to designs that can be wrapped around the human torso. This brilliance in reducing things of everyday life to patterns and then adapting these patterns to the human form is one of the high points of Japanese textile design.

Patterns vary for men and women, for young and old. Children's *yukata* have still different blue and white designs. Fashions change in *yukata* patterns each year, but the glory of the blue and white tradition always reaches a peak when people dress in *yukata*, bright *obi* around women's waists and smart tie-dyed sashes tied low around slim male hips, wooden clogs on bare feet, and go out to celebrate summer: fireworks, festivals, and outdoor concerts. The blue and white *yukata* is loved not only for brilliance of design, but also because it is a garment of recreation and fun.

Although techniques in *yukata* dyeing and coloring have become sophisticated and advanced, dyeing is still a labor-intensive process that entails many pairs of hands. And despite refinements and new color schemes, dyers and customers alike always seem to return to the basic combination of dark blue and white.

The *yukata* fabric comes in rolls about 11.8 meters long and 36 centimeters wide, which can be used for any design project calling for textiles. Covered tea boxes, photo albums, picture frames — all look striking in bold blue and white. Quilters have found a new frontier in blue and white *yukata* material as well, producing ingenious new designs and combinations that expand the boundaries of this hard-working textile.

Left: Spiral-pattern *yukata* drying outside at the Nibe house. On the floor, a pair of padded indigo slippers awaits the laundress.

Right: A New England four poster transplanted to a Tokyo house is dressed up with variously patterned lengths of blue and white *yukata* cotton. An assortment of cushions and an early 20th-century festival jacket with a design of tied paper fortunes provide a fresh contrast to the lace coverlet.

Previous page: A summery linen quilt cover dresses the *futon* bed in the Nibe guest room. A *yukata* has been left out for the guest to slip on, and another hangs on the clothing rack. An ink-painting screen and an arrangement of wildflowers in a ceramic *hibachi* give spirit to the lacquered alcove.

A blue and white kitchen

makes sense. Inside, outside, topsy-turvy at times, it may go from calm to chaos with the regularity of the meals of the day, but behind the scenes the logic of color helps maintain balance and harmony. Blue and white hand towels placed hastily in drawers seem to form themselves into well-ordered stacks; blue and white tiles placed around a stove or sink create an easy order. A cheerful blue sink makes washing up less of a chore. Even mismatched Imari and other dishes piled high in cupboards or towering on counters come together if they are all blue and white.

The kitchen today is more lived in than any other room in a house. This is the place where families and friends gather to cook, talk, and eat. Filling a center of activity with unpretentious Japanese blue and white ceramics creates a calm and order that welcome all who enter. People can be themselves against this nothing-fancy background setting. Best of all, the innate order of the blue and white combination, even in its wildest patterns and pairings, keeps chaos at bay in today's hectic world.

Right: Blue and white bottoms. Clean-up time features the chance to turn over some lovely pieces of Imari — old, new, valuable and not — and see what different chops and marks are painted there. The other side of an Imari plate tells a whole different story. The Imari shards in the old goldfish bowl were found on neighborhood walks.
Below: Everyday family rice bowls. Mends add flavor.

Left: Stacks of blue and white bowls ready for lunch. No need for everything to coordinate. Mix, match, juxtapose, and let the colors clash and patterns crash where they will.

Below: 19th-century crane-shaped plates and sake pourers set out for a small dinner. Behind, a traditional glass storage jar keeps homemade ginger cookies handy.

Above: Surrounded by blue and white dragonfly tiles hand-painted by Kaoru Fujisaka for Tokyo's Blue and White, a four-burner stove becomes an enchanted place to cook.

Right: Chaos in the kitchen! Party preparations mean food, flowers, cooking, decorating, all happening at the same time. Only the theme of blue and white offers calm amid the storm.

Right: Blue and white delight in the specially designed kitchen of Rêves de Vie, the innovative restaurant of Patrice Julien in Tokyo's Centre des Arts Français. Brilliant cobalt-blue stove and refrigerator, made to order in Japan, catch the eye, while the Mexican checkerboard tiles play with it. French and Japanese aesthetics combine in a kitchen whose glory is in its attention to detail. The creator and chef scours flea markets to find ceramics and other accents for the tables, walls, and counters. And everyday, spicy aromas mix with the visual feast to assure the diner of a meal to remember from a blue and white kitchen.

Choosing porcelains is like

choosing a spouse. You want to be able to live with and have dinner with your choice night after night, without growing bored. Similarly, your blue and white porcelain should speak to you. Perfection isn't necessary, nor does expense guarantee a good match. So how to explain why I choose what I choose?

If I were to identify one outstanding criteron for what draws my eye, it would be design. When I am roaming the flea markets or browsing through antique shops, playful, whimsical motifs invariably catch my attention. Unexpected patterns pull me up short — bats flitting over rabbits, a plate that is half blue and half white with a raised turtle design on one side and a raised crane on the other, or a plate in the shape of a turnip outlined in blue. Such startling originality stands out from a Japanese blue and white tradition that is largely predictable. This does not mean that all the blue and white pieces I own have to be attention-grabbers, but a few of them have to make me smile, or make me sit up straight, or better still, help everyone enjoy the food.

The history of blue and white is there for those who want to

Left: The blue and white dishes in the kitchen of Harumi Nibe bear witness to a keen eye that recognized classic design and fine quality even on pieces bought years ago on a slender budget. Today, Nibe-san's fine collection is a fitting stage for her inventive cuisine.
Below: Purple hydrangeas in a whimsical *hibachi* with designs of plovers and waves.

Right: An original dishcloth stitched by Kazumi Yoshida against a backdrop of blue and white porcelain tiles.

Below: Only the best ingredients are used in the kitchen of the Rêves de Vie restaurant, in Tokyo's Shirogane district. Carefully chosen blue and white ceramics and cottons give flavor. Here, a spatter-pattern bowl with a maple-leaf motif, an assortment of tin spoons on a bold blue and white hand towel, and, under the spatula, an unusual crescent-shaped tile.

study it, although, in fact, remarkably little is written about it in English. Korean potters brought blue and white techniques from the mainland to Kyushu at the beginning of the seventeenth century. For a while potters and patrons had to be content with inferior Japanese copies of Korean originals. Just when Japanese potters developed a sense of themselves and diverged from Korean prototypes is uncertain. Orders from Europe originally went to China, where the porcelains were superior, but wars in China brought the business to Japan and resulted in the development of Japanese export ware, blue and white porcelains totally different from those made for the domestic market. While Chinese Ming-dynasty and Korean Yi-dynasty pieces are impressive, something simple and strong speaks out from Japanese porcelains, making them original statements apart from and, to my mind, above their Chinese but close to their Korean antecedents.

What is distinctive about Japanese blue and white porcelain? Themes are straighforward, grasses perhaps, or flowers, waves and birds, images of nature. But the observation is exquisite, the ability to capture a moment on a small curved surface is unparalleled. As collector and dealer Susumu

Right, above: Tools of the kitchen trade fill a convenient small-sized blue and white stenciled *hibachi* with a scene of travelers crossing a wooden bridge. Next to it, a snowflake-shaped tile waits for hot things to be set down.
Right, below: Okinawan pots fresh from the kiln of Tsunehide Shimabukuro.
Below: Lily-pad-shaped tile from an old bathhouse with a bat and autumn grasses motif found at a flea market.

Kakitani has observed, Japanese artists had to have the eye of an ant to be able to fit universal themes and motifs on the side of a small cup. The deft distillation of what they saw around them is the greatest gift of Japanese craftsmen.

Color is also an issue when I choose blue and white. I know this is old-fashioned, and probably due to the fact that when I started collecting, Edo-period (1603–1868) blue and white Imari was readily available, but I prefer lighter, more

The pleasure of blue and white comes from having a piece that fits you and your way of living. Maybe the blue and white plate is the perfect shape for serving your special recipe for ginger pork or chilled tofu, or maybe it holds your correspondence or pins on the bureau. Like a husband or wife, it suits you, and promises a lifetime of enjoyment together.

subtle colors to the brighter cobalt blues of the later nineteenth century. Although these are very popular now, as are the stenciled patterns that became common around the same time, I am drawn to softer colors and less distinct designs because they are more retiring when serving food and don't call for attention like the later pieces. But that is all a matter of taste.

On the table

is where blue and white ceramics truly shine. The simplest fare becomes elegant with the artful use of a few dramatic Imari dishes.

When I set tables, I begin with the tablecloth. This forms the backdrop, the canvas. A clean old bedcover perhaps, in a *karakusa,* arabesque, pattern, or an indigo carrying cloth placed on the diagonal. Serve salad on rectangular blue and white plates, add a casual arrangement of indigo-purple flowers, fill a team of tall glasses with roughly rolled cloth napkins, and even the most basic fare will assume gourmet dimensions.

Blue and white porcelain

When I began collecting and was hit with my blue and white addiction, I began to make weekly rounds of the antique shops to look for blue and white porcelain — *sometsuke.* This was long before the advent of flea markets, in the golden days when things were cheap and the yen was 360 to the American dollar. Good things were commonplace. Even if you didn't know what you were doing, you could come home with some remarkable finds.

Unwittingly, a collection was born. Actually, it multiplied so fast I feared reprimands from my mother-in-law when she came for dinner to find yet another new set of plates in use. One evening I thought the game was up, but her words turned out to be wise advice. "Now that you are collecting blue and white dishes so seriously," she laughed, "it might be good to concentrate on other shapes, not just round ones. Round is too symmetrical. Look for oblongs, hexagonals," she advised, "try flutes and leaf shapes." How right she was. The round dishes began to bore me once my eye became more discerning.

Back then, even a beginner could stumble onto amazing pieces. Today, it helps to know something about blue and white porcelain.

Left: At a garden party held in Tokyo, simplicity reigns in the spontaneous mismatching of blue and white Imari bowls, a pottery teapot filled with cherry blossoms, and everyday spotted teacups on a vintage homespun *kasuri* tablecloth.
Below: Collector's dream: a stack of old Imari bowls and platters waiting to be used.

The Japanese blue and white ceramic tradition was born with the discovery of white porcelain clay (kaolin) in Kyushu, southern Japan, in 1616 by Ri Sampei, a naturalized Korean. Many Kyushu pottery kilns converted to high-fire porcelain production, and with the fall of the Ming dynasty in China in 1644, Dutch traders brought European orders for porcelain to Japan. In a startlingly short time, Japanese porcelain grew highly sophisticated and developed its own distinctive character.

Japanese porcelain vocabulary

Sometsuke is a generic term for blue and white cobalt underglaze porcelains.

Arita is cobalt underglaze porcelain, named after the district where it was first made.

Imari designates underglaze porcelain, originally blue and white, produced in the Arita district on the island of Kyushu from early in the seventeeth century. It is named after the port from which it was sent to other parts of Japan, such as Nagasaki, to be loaded onto Dutch ships headed for Europe. Arita and Imari are largely synonymous.

Shoki Imari, "early" Imari, was made from 1616 to 1650. It is not often seen today.

Ko Imari, "old" Imari, is porcelain of blue cobalt underglaze on a gray-white ground. It can also refer to overglazed, colored enamel porcelains of the time. Produced from about 1650 until 1750, Ko Imari is rare and highly prized today.

Export ware describes Japanese porcelains made to European tastes, ordered by traders of the Dutch East India Company for the European market. These are characterized by bright, enamel colors.

Inban, designs stenciled onto ceramics that were smaller and more detailed than the free, loose designs of hand-brushed pieces, became popular in the second half of the nineteenth century. The Meiji Restoration opened the country in 1868, and new methods to step up production were introduced to meet growing demand for porcelains of every kind, including *hibachi,* which had heretofore been made of wood or metal.

Above: Spotted bowls with red lacquer lids are a family heirloom, a treasure received from a kind and savvy mother-in-law. Sake pourers serve as candle stands.

Left: Old Imari bowls, gathered over many years of collecting, reflect the soft colors of a patched collage of stenciled hemp fabric used as a tablecloth. The piece in front is a small lidded rice bowl.

Ultimately, the essense of collecting blue and white porcelains is finding plates and bowls and cups that appeal to you. Don't worry about pieces not matching. On the table, it's best to play with, and celebrate, the endless variety of blue and white. Mix things up. Begin by throwing together clashing textile patterns to create surface interest. Place mats, table runners, even a long narrow piece of blue and white *yukata* fabric will look original when crossed with interwoven strips of cloth that mark each place setting. Try blue and white striped *tenugui* hand towels as napkins. *Tenugui* are long and narrow and sit nicely across the lap. Don't forget place mats, blue and white frames for your dishes. I try to put something original on the table every time I entertain. It's an energizing challenge, and the effort can bring a new twist to a party and inspire the evening.

Then bring on the dishes. It's more interesting if every-

Above: Humor, beauty, and a bit of the unexpected combine on Martyne Kupciunas' luncheon table set with a mix of old blue and white dishes on recycled place mats and sparked with napkins rolled in red rings of knotted grosgrain cloth.
Left: Detail of three layers of rags stitched together as a cleaning cloth, but here used as a surprise place mat.
Facing page: An Okinawan institution — the Daiichi Hotel in Naha. Breakfast here presents a display of Okinawan craft and culture on the table and dish after dish of seasonal food to feed your daydreams long after the feast has ended.

one has a different plate. If you are worried because a dignified prince and princess are coming for dinner, relax — they'll have more fun if you don't try to live by their rules. Be original. Use your dishes in new ways — pour some dipping sauce for spinach samosas in individual sake cups. Pick some wild chrysanthemums or some autumn grasses and place them in blue and white bottles lined up on the table. Use an old Imari bath tile as a hot plate. If you keep blue and white as the unifying force, aesthetic harmony will prevail. Then feel free to expand and express your own taste and spirit within that blue and white theme. This is the essence of blue and white living.

Above: Teacup irreverently served on stitched country footwear.
Left: Prized antique Windsor chairs around an 18th-century English oak table (all from the Sanshiro Ikeda collection) form a serene backdrop for a Japanese tea party for two. Barley tea and rice balls await on a vintage striped horse rein.

Right: Indigo mosquito netting weaves a spell over an antique Spanish table wrapped in blue and white striped horse textiles. Dishes stacked on the table issue an easy invitation to help yourself and have a good time.
Below: Old Imari sake-cup rests reborn as candle stands.

Above: The simplest meal comes alive with the use of a strong textile, here, a double *kasuri futon* cover.

Left: A grouping of blue and white stacked dishes, a worn roof tile, and antique wooden candlesticks on a *tansu*. The table is reflected in the unusual lacquer mirror with a mysterious carved calligraphy frame, inviting us to join in the meal.

Right: Set a blue and white table and the rest takes care of itself. The job is done here with a *shibori futon* cover spread as a tablecloth and a mix of blue and white dishes. An Imari bowl filed with azaleas is the crowning blaze of color.

Below: Teatime at the Nibe house means interesting food and unexpected combinations of food and dish and cloth.

Left: Amazing grace. Even sandwiches have dignity when served in this timeless room in Sanshiro Ikeda's museum house. Arranged on an old blue and white *sashiko furoshiki* and accompanied by an Okinawan basket (originally for hanging overhead to keep provisions cool and aired), the simplest fare takes on elegant proportions.

Left: Tadayoshi Ikemoto's whimsical teapot with black-eyed Susans sets the tone for lunch outside. A rectangular basket serves as a tabletop.
Below left: Spaghetti squash forms a brilliant contrast against a platter of cobalt blue and white.
Below: Rice served on green leaves is picture perfect.
Right: A spur-of-the-moment lunch at Harumi Nibe's house becomes an affair to remember under a colorful canopy of antique trappings originally used in Tohoku to decorate horses.

Left: Here rustic and sophisticated come together and speak of good taste. A large painting by English artist Lucy Jones and a 17th-century carved wood Burmese Buddha bless a lunch on the run. Fresh flowers repeat the yellow and green accents on an antique French country table set with an old *tsutsugaki* textile with a pattern of *noshi,* folded paper used to decorate a gift.

Above right: An arabesque-pattern *furoshiki,* the textile predecessor of the paper bag, becomes a cheerful picnic blanket on an enchanted Okinawan beach.

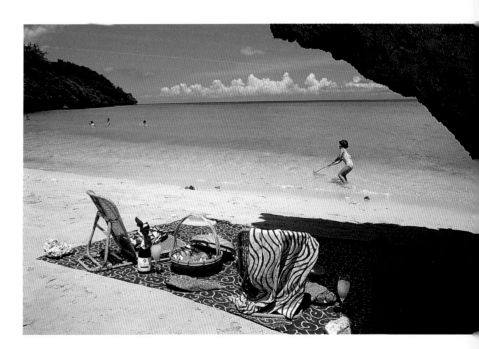

Above: Served on a handmade Okinawan basket, simple fare makes a memorable alfresco picnic created with sun, sea and thee, blue and white.

A story in a *soba* cup

Yoshihiro Takishita of the House of Antiques in Kamakura advises: It is better to have one beautiful *soba* cup (used for dipping *soba* noodles) with a minor chip on the base than a perfect piece that is ugly. For me, this is the most basic principle. As for specifics, I recommend collectors look for the following:

Shape: Older Imari *soba* cups tend to have a high "foot." The base of the earliest Imari is narrow and tall and recedes at the bottom.

Design: Common design motifs appear throughout three centuries of blue and white Imari. For example, *tako karakusa,* spiral arabesque designs, and *karakusa,* Chinese arabesque designs, have been around for ages. But despite the endless repetition of such designs, subtle changes made in each period help identify when a cup was made. In the Meiji era, for example, patterns began to be applied through stencils rather than brushed on, resulting in more intricate and "perfect" designs.

Color: The coloration of blue and white Imari is achieved with cobalt underglaze. Natural cobalt, Chinese, Japanese, or Korean, has a grayish cast, so early pieces had a grayish-blue tone. During the Meiji Restoration, a chemically pure "German Blue" cobalt was imported from Europe, and after 1868, other shades of blue appeared, making later pieces more brilliant in color.

Touch: The final important detail is how the *soba* cup, or any piece of Imari for that matter, feels in the hand. How is it to drink from? If it conveys a feeling of natural balance, of completeness, it is a well-crafted cup.

How to develop an eye? Go to museums and galleries to see good examples of Imari cups (although they may be hard to find in museums, since they are often considered unworthy). This will help you develop your knowledge and taste. Identifying the age of a piece is not that important. The things to look for are shape, design, color, feel, and last of all, condition. Trust the dealer who tells you where the crack or chip is. In porcelain, very little surreptitious repair work is done, and often a sticker will warn against a crack or chip on even a slightly damaged piece.

Right: Patterned Edo-period *soba* cups from the collection of Susumu Kakitani.

Right: Blue and white bubbles over on this table set for a festive dinner party. Stripes and spots combine close to the boiling point, but never explode as they would were it any other color combination. Old Imari plates, new plates, two contrasting *kasuri* textiles overlaid as tablecloths, and new tie-dyed napkins create layer upon layer of blue and white. The wildflowers were arranged by Harumi Nibe. The room is enclosed by *shoji,* Japanese paper screens, on three sides. In the background hangs a 17th-century Genji-Heike battle screen.

Previous page: On the veranda of a converted temple in Matsumoto, a spontaneous picnic of what is available has more energy than anything long planned and elaborately staged. Rags and baskets and blue and white make the difference.

Right and below: In the garden of Kosoen, lunch on the rocks. Free-flowing indigo textiles and wine chilling in a small *hibachi* add to the exuberance that indigo and a blue and white sky can create. Standing on guard is a low-fired clay pig incense burner, used to discourage insects.

Blue and white skies

need to be celebrated. Call some friends, run to the local market, and think simple. For a picnic outdoors, the key is in the presentation, which should be casual and unfussy. If food is served on blue and white platters among comfortable textiles spread out on the deck — small indigo patchwork quilts, an old blue and white checkered dog blanket, a large ragweave rug — the picnic will shine. Scatter some leaves from nearby trees on the plates or arrange them in hand-painted paper lanterns. For a crowning touch, stretch a gauze indigo-dipped canopy overhead to shade the revelers below.

Left, below: Friends and family gather on the deck to enjoy a blue and white lunch. Above, indigo-dyed gauze reflects the color of the sky and protects from the relentless sun. Below, blue and white *zabuton* help make an impromptu picnic a party to remember. **Clockwise from top left:** Even an old blue and white dog blanket works as a tablecloth; Imari bowls and platters filled with simple summer food; a ceramic incense burner for mosquito coils; hand-painted paper lanterns by Takako Fukuchi of Blue and White; grilled sausages accented with green leaves; dessert stacked in an old two-tiered basket.

Indigo threads

Some mornings seem to come directly from the indigo pot. Pale blue washes of sky running down to triple-dipped indigo mountains. In the garden of Kosoen in Ome, Tokyo, newly dyed cloths — bolts of inky blue, fresh from the indigo vats — mimic the colors of the morning. The pot design on the large *noren* in the center is the dyer's logo.

Indigo textiles were the fabric of the country-

side in Japan, created from a life in close harmony with mountains, valleys, and seas. Rugged, durable kimono and work clothes were made of what was available, first bast fibers, hemp, barks, grass, and tree fibers. When cotton was introduced, around the fifteenth century, that warmer, softer fiber became the fiber of choice for spinning, weaving, and dyeing.

Once there was a loom in every farmhouse and fisherman's cottage. Each household created its own clothes, quilts, towels. Farmers harvested indigo from the fields, and frothy indigo-dye vats were a common sight. From today's affluence, we look back and see that the beauty of those blue textiles was born from the hard ground of poverty. People then had no choice but to make do as they could. Today, choice is the opiate of the people, and the techniques that remain do not have the strength born of necessity and hard work that shone in the old indigo compositions. Bits of brilliance still remain in *yukata* patterns and the works of stencil and tie-dye dyers. But where is the lyricism of the nineteenth-century textiles? I keep going back to flea markets and antique shops, because it's those old textiles that speak most eloquently.

Right: The hands of Shokichi Watanabe of Gujo Hachiman in Gifu show different stages of his craft, from tying the cloth in knots to resist the dye, to hanging out his newly dyed *shibori,* to dipping the cloth to be dyed, and undoing the knots.
Below: Dried indigo waiting to be used.

Indigo is the most durable and readily available natural color for application to textiles, and people the world over have used it since time immemorial. It has been treasured and respected particularly in China, India, Indonesia, Guatemala, Ecuador, France, Holland, Nigeria, Mali, the Cameroons, and Japan, where the indigo tradition is strong (although today it is supported everywhere by slender threads, and Japan is no exception).

Japan's indigo crop is produced predominantly by a cartel of four farms in Tokushima, on the island of Shikoku. Distribution is fixed, since production is limited. Costs are so fearsome that many dyers mix real indigo with various chemical blends, although many also claim they use only the real thing. A few dyers still grow and process their own indigo, but most dyers buy sacks of fermented indigo leaves formed into "balls."

White is an important ingredient in the indigo recipes of all these dyers. White, the absence of color, is the perfect counterpoint to the power of indigo shades.

Blue jeans are today's response to the ancient wisdom of indigo. Now dyed with chemical dyes, but still possessing the irrepressible charisma of everyday indigo work clothes, worn and weathered blue jeans echo the magic hold that indigo has had over man.

Left: Tamiko Makishi preparing silk in her weaving studio in Okinawa.

Left, below: Unusual *shimenawa,* a sacred New Year's decoration, on a cotton banner hangs behind a backpack basket filled with balls of twisted cloth rope used for hanging banners and other country tasks.

Below: A clump of indigo *kasuri* threads becomes a mysterious knotted sculpture.

Following page: Indigo entrance. A 19th-century *tsutsugaki* padded sleeping kimono with an unusual *daikon* radish design, a fertility symbol, hangs above a 19th-century Imari bowl, a handmade *washi* container filled with wild grass, and a pair of stone wild boar.

Indigo craftsmen

Shokichi Watanabe, a prefectural cultural asset in Gujo Hachiman in Gifu, has been dyeing indigo for decades. He first dips his textiles in liquid ash lye to produce a stately indigo only shades away from black. This is a traditional way of keeping the indigo fast and deep.

Kosoen, in Ome in the far west of Tokyo, produces a youthful blue that whistles with fresh air and sunshine. This shop uses gradations of blue and is particularly good on the lighter registers. Kosoen is open to visitors, who are welcome to see how indigo is dyed and try it themselves.

Hiroyuki Shindo of Miyama in Kyoto Prefecture is the master of a glorious indigo for all seasons that he has developed over thirty years of dyeing. His soulful, rich textiles are grounded in the earth and yet have the gentle touch of his cultured mind. Likewise, his designs have the grace and playfulness of a man whose cycle of living is in perfect balance.

Kenji Tanaka's designs are cerebral, his spheres of indigo inspired by planets and other celestial phenomena. He blends fiber and tone to produce translucent *noren* and wall hangings. His wife, **Aiko Tanaka**, weaves indigo textiles that she makes into kimono. Her clean lines and weaves deftly display the endless variety of indigo — greens, grays, blues, lavenders.

Seizo Ishikawa, a vegetable farmer in Saitama Prefecture, produces only one indigo vat a year for his annual indigo exhibition in the Saitama City Museum. He makes only what he needs as a personal challenge, not for commercial reasons. This gives his work total honesty and an artistic and intellectual force that is powerful and captivating.

Matsubara Somekojo, four brothers, sons of a Living National Treasure stencil cutter, apply sophisticated designs to fine hemps and *yukata* cottons and dye them an ethereal shade of blue.

An Indigo primer

Blue and white answers to demands for textiles for daily life were stunning, ingenious compositions. Countless variations were produced by creative hands working within the context of materials provided by nature — bast fibers, cotton, hemp, silk, and indigo.

Sashiko stitchery is a simple running stitch applied to the surface of a textile. Originally *sashiko* was used to reinforce fabrics and make them sturdy and durable, but the concomitant patterns that evolved from practical needs produced clothes of great lyricism for rice fields and battlefields. *Sashiko* features geometric designs and was used in carrying cloths, hand towels, work clothes, and undergarments for armor.

Tsutsugaki technique involves freely drawn designs that are applied with paste resist squeezed through a conical tube. The textile is then dipped in indigo and other colors are applied by brush later. Country dyers produced *tsutsugaki* textiles, often with mythical and auspicious designs, as bedding, wrapping cloths, banners, and celebratory textiles for weddings, births, and other important events. The freshness and imagination in the work of *tsutsugaki* dyers has made *tsutsugaki* among the most sought-after textiles. But gone, alas, are the masters who produced the textile flights of fancy of the latter nineteenth and early twentieth centuries.

Shibori, known as the material with a memory, is a family of techniques (including tie-dye) involving shaping, binding, and tying areas of fabric to keep them undyed when the cloth is dipped into a dye vat. Left unironed, a *shibori* fabric retains the puckers and pleats of the technique employed, giving a textile three-dimensional texture as well as design. Different *shibori* techniques create amazing geometric as well as figurative compositions. In its heyday, handmade *shibori* constituted the most remarkable textile creations in Japan and was highly sought after for its subtle yet vigorous designs.

Kasuri is also known as ikat, the Indonesian term for resist-binding threads prior to dyeing and weaving to produce predetermined designs in both the weft and warp. *Kasuri* was widely used in Japan for farm clothing, carrying cloths, and bedding. Today good indigo *kasuri* cloth is still being produced in Kyushu (in Kurume), in Shikoku, and in Hiroshima.

Katazome stencil dyeing has been used for hundreds of years as a way of applying design to surface. Stencils made of *washi* are cut with the desired design. After they are treated with persimmon tannin and reinforced with a fine silk mesh, they are laid on the textile surface and the paste resist — different dyers use different recipes — is forced through the cut openings. Stencil dyeing is still widely used today in *yukata* and *tenugui* dyeing.

Sakiori results when old, tattered textiles are torn into strips and recycled by being woven into ragweave sashes, quilt covers, or even floor coverings.

Blues in the house.

Blue is a strong color. Many Japanese textiles have such strength in color, design, and dyeing that restraint is required to use them. A deep blue-black indigo textile, for example, can overpower other colors and combinations. But with care and a little artistic sensibility, blue and white textiles can provide your most elegant decorative statement. One humorous indigo *tsutsugaki* kimono or wall hanging, with a freehand paste-resist design of jumping carp, frolicking *shishi,* temple dogs or lions, or swimming turtles will set a playful tone for an entire room. A single, soft-colored patchwork quilt used as a rug can provide a beautiful backdrop for a simple antique child's chair, turning a neglected corner of a dark room into a study in light and pattern. Don't be afraid to throw several different textiles into the mix. Abundance provides impact. Juxtaposed *kasuri* patterns start the action and set a table in motion. Even a subtly textured *sashiko* quilted work coat, with its quiet interplay of tones, patterns, and shades, becomes part of a vibrant still life when displayed behind a pair of smiling wooden *shishi* and an unusual candle stand.

Right: Two carved wooden *shishi* stand guard with a sacred jewel-shaped candle stand and a well-weathered *sashiko* coat.
Below: Antique Windsor child's chair draped with a *tsutsugaki* child's towel from Izumo, whose auspicious symbols and colors are believed to protect the child from evil.

The language of design and pattern

Pattern is everywhere in Japan. The curve of a leaf, the swirl of a wave, spots of rain, the sway of bamboo, all are reduced to their essence to embellish the surface of textile, ceramic, metal, or paper. Many patterns used in Japan come from Korean or Chinese antecedents, but the lyrical Japanese observation of nature, the keen eye for the fleeting moment, the delight in detail, allow craftsmen to capture and transpose nature's motifs into designs of unique eloquence that set the patterns of Japan apart.

Once you begin identifying patterns in one medium such as cloth or clay, you will recognize them across the Japanese craft spectrum. Turtles and waves, pine trees and cranes, plum blossoms, checks, stripes, lightning, clouds, and the like form the common art vocabulary of the entire country. They all are traditionally associated with meanings and stories, which were close to folklore. Many of the most popular motifs are also auspicious: for example, giant radishes (fertility), bamboo (longevity), and rice (fecundity). Other patterns with implied messages are chrysanthemums, peonies, butterflies, dragonflies, bats, and the twelve Chinese-zodiac animals, each with its own characteristics.

Decoration by Japanese craftsmen has reached heights unsurpassed anywhere in the world, yet letting materials themselves speak, without added embellishment, is also given as much admiration as decoration. In the language of Japanese pattern and design, it is the freshness of approach that matters.

Left: A *tsutsugaki* of long-living tortoises shares good fortune with visitors to the Hoksbergen house, with a carving of three monkeys who speak, hear, see no evil.
Right, from top: Pattern parade. Indigo textile with alternating bands of fine pattern, including chrysanthemums and water; lion's hair; blue and white checks; swimming carp.

Choosing old indigo textiles

Words of wisdom from Tadashi Morita of Morita Antiques in Tokyo.

Colors. *Blue:* I don't know why, but Japan seems to avoid bright, basic colors. There are many different shades of blue: reddish, purplish, blackish (which gives the strange impression that the fabric hasn't been used), yellowish, almost-green, pale sky blue. But none is really bright. I prefer washed-out blue, a faded powder blue. Real lovers of antique cloth will look for a touch of white between blue threads.
White: I never pay much attention to white, but when I choose a washed-out blue, the white areas will usually be a dirty white, not pure.
Other colors: In *tsutsugaki,* natural colors are sometimes mixed with chemical dyes.

Design. Look for an interesting design on the textile, one with some charm or power. I prefer floral motifs in *tsutsugaki.* I have never seen a truly top-quality tiger or phoenix. Textile designs are not professional artworks — otherwise they would not be folk art! But even if a piece has been rendered by a folk artist, it can still be a beautiful, collectible work if it has some humor or whimsy to it.

Texture. I prefer thick cotton to other materials, and ideally the threads should be homespun and woven by hand — and dyed by hand, of course.

Age. I judge the age of a textile by experience, so I can't give others a simple formula for how to determine age. But it's useful to remember that while cotton and indigo first came to Japan about one thousand years ago, they were subsequently lost for many centuries. Indigo was originally used only to dye hemp. Cotton was reintroduced to Japan 400 years ago and became popular because it accepts indigo dye readily.

Mending. I don't mind at all if a textile is mended. In fact, patches and mends sometimes give more meaning and feeling to a piece.

Left: Textile art. Sanshiro Ikeda wears a padded sleeping kimono with an auspicious crane and turtle design that invokes the spirituality of the crane and the longevity of the turtle. The masterful interaction of the cranes around the family crest symbol is a brilliant example of an anonymous dyer's mastery of his medium. (A front view of Ikeda-san and the kimono can be found on page 8.)
Below: Keiko Nomoto, a textile and indigo artist and kimono devotee, stitching one of her original *sashiko* pieces.

Out of the blue.

There's nothing like it! The thrill of the hunt at the flea market. The energy of the sudden find. You spot. You bargain. You bring it home. But when you get home with your treasure, you realize you have a smelly blue and white textile or a blue and white ceramic pitted with the dirt of the ages.

So hit the tubs! Man the soaps, the detergents, the bleaches, and the brushes! If it's a cotton or hemp textile, immerse it in cold water with Woolite, or in Japan, Monogen. It can soak for some time while the grime emerges. (But be careful if your textile has other colors present, for they can be fugitive, particularly the volatile reds. Don't let them sit in water for any time at all.) If it is dark indigo and doesn't seem to have been washed before, throw a half cup of vinegar or salt into the cold-water bath to stabilize the color. I like to see the excess indigo cloud the water and swim away, leaving a gentler and deeper blue in the textile. The joy of hanging a newly clean *futon* cover or kimono on the line and watching it dry is indescribable. The original energy and brilliance of the textile have been restored. The richness of usage and mellowness of age deepen with each washing. Threads become distinct, and the

Right: Setsuko Shinoda stops to cool herself at the town well in Gujo Hachiman in Gifu Prefecture. She wears a splashy indigo *yukata* in a Chinese bellflower pattern by Shokichi Watanabe. Hanging above the well is a *shimenawa,* a sacred rope.
Below: The *noren* of the Hotel Kikunoyu in Matsumoto, Nagano Prefecture, greets all passers-by.

Left: Hung from tall bamboo poles lashed together, a long, heroic Kintaro banner adds drama to a temple meditation tower outside Matsumoto that overlooks the Japan Alps. (Momotaro is a popular mythical boy hero of Japan, known for his strength.)

Right, above: Washday blues. Blue and white laundry drying in the Okinawan sun — kimono, bathing suits, and *shibori* cloths used for everything from carrying picnic provisions to drying children just out of the surf.

Right, below: A design-perfect horse trapping invigorates the concrete of an ultramodern Tokyo house. On the left, a flower arrangement under way in a blue and white porcelain *hibachi*.

texture and depth of the fabric are wonderful to see when they emerge. You have released the textile from years of neglect, and your reward is the pleasure of owning a shining old/new piece imbued with the spirit of the maker who wove or dyed it years before.

Washing is equally satisfying with blue and white ceramics. Take them home and plunge them into a tub of hot water and suds. If normal dish detergent isn't strong enough for the deep dirt, try a cleanser or bleach. This applies only to blue and white porcelains. Polychrome overglaze ceramics must be handled more carefully. Blue and white is all underglaze and so can withstand more robust — but still gentle — treatment. If all the dirt is not removed on the first wash, leave the dishes to soak in hot water and a gentle bleach for as long as it takes to remove the grime. Then pick them up one by one and scrub each vigorously with a soft brush. Some delicacy is required when you wash textiles, but the ceramics can stand a fair amount of persistence.

You will be dazzled by the transformation that has taken place. You sensed your treasure's power and potential at the flea market. With simple washing, the blues and whites have come clean and the acuity of your eye and rightness of your instinct are confirmed! Freshly scrubbed, your ceramics and textiles sparkle in their brightness and new-found energy. The only thing more satisfying than discovering treasures at the market is bringing them home and returning them to their original splendor with soap and water, a brush, an iron, and care.

Banner days are magical.

May 5 is Boys' Day in Japan and celebrates the sons of the family. An indigo Boys' Day banner hung outside lends an air of excitement to the celebration and announces the season to all. At left, Sanshiro Ikeda celebrates his eighty-sixth birthday with a lively *tsutsugaki* banner. Banners such as this are traditionally used on holidays, festivals, and other special occasions (such as observances at shrines or sumo tournaments) to communicate a message of time and season and celebration. Wraparound banners (rather than the kind that are hung) are used to mark boundaries for gatherings of various kinds, including festivals, funerals, and groundbreakings.

Tenugui.

Without this humble hand towel, Japan would never have made it to where it is today! Some 30 by 90 centimeters in length, the multipurpose cotton *tenugui* is dyed with simple, offhand designs — a family crest, a checkerboard border, a few casual bamboo leaves. Charming, spontaneous compositions such as these make this mundane textile an instant work of art, unsung and unheralded, but splendid nevertheless. Best of all, it is beautiful *and* useful. Hand towel, sweatband, scrub cloth, rag, dish towel — no Japanese at work would be without one. Check a craftsman's or carpenter's belt, head, or pocket and you will find a *tenugui* tied, twisted, or folded there. This book certainly wouldn't have happened without them. We use *tenugui* to mop our brows and dry our hands, scrub ceramics, wipe tables, wrap bundles. Whenever there is a job to be done, *tenugui* are there, helping.

You used to be able to determine a man's profession by the way he knotted his *tenugui.* When going on location, Yutaka Satoh, our magic photographer, always packs his camera gear, his *tenugui,* and his clothes, in that order. His own personal *tenugui,* dyed with a charming rendering of his distinctive camera, serves as a kind of autograph. He gives it out as an eye-snapping calling card at festivals he participates in and at business meetings.

Tenugui used to be given by tradesmen at year-end and at the summer gift-giving season as advertisement, thanks, and wish for continued patronage. They are given less frequently these days, alas, though trendy shops specializing in traditional Japanese clothing have

Left: Patterns sing and shout on this cotton *tenugui*.
Right: Take your pick from the bare-branch towel bars offering a whole range of *tenugui* in the Nibe bathroom. Blue and white beckoning cats are by Yu Kobayashi.

come to recognize their beauty and now sell them as the art-to-wear and art-at-work pieces they are.

As surprising as it is to visitors, this simple length of cloth is also a bath towel — a narrow one, indeed. Most hot springs in Japan give guests a *tenugui*. This is supposed to provide cover as you walk naked into the steaming public bath. Shield whatever parts you choose! One friend cleverly suggested that the best place to put it was over one's head. Once you are in the bath, however, the *tenugui* is your washcloth and brush. Wring it out once you are done, then use it to wipe yourself dry. Remarkable efficiency and conservation of resources, all in one small hand-dyed cloth.

Japan has taught me that no person should ever be without a *tenugui*. You never know when you will need one — to dry your hands in a land without paper towels, to wrap some books or flowers, to wipe your bicycle seat after a rainstorm.

Tenugui are quick to wash and quick to dry, and they become better with use. Well-laundered and worn *tenugui* are far more pleasing than freshly dyed new ones. Use them once and then wash in soap and water or just rinse them out and hang to dry on a windowpane or similar flat place. They will dry flat and need no ironing. The *tenugui* — don't leave home without one!

Left: Blues in the bath, inside and out. Overlooking an ever-changing sea and sky, this bath is a dip in paradise. Soak and dream, and when you're done, a fresh *yukata* and slippers will wrap you in blue and white comfort.
Below: *Tenugui* hung on a small lacquered rack. A rustic beckoning cat waves welcome.

Right: A kimono made by weaver Tamiko Makishi dries in her bathroom. The cool *yukata* hung over the bathtub is ready to wear.

Right, below: A Seiji Nibe original creature made from found iron serves as a fey toilet-paper holder. Another recycled creature sits on a *tenugui* on the toilet tank. A *yukata*-fabric spiral rug on the floor and various pieces of Imari arranged on the shelf add blue and white panache.

Above: An all-white bath is enlivened with Japanese blue and white checked towels and small *hibachi.* The tissue box is covered in *yukata* material.

Facing page: In the bathroom of a restaurant, a charming French-made sink and tiles are complemented with *tenugui* towels hung on a bamboo dowel. An old striped horse rein frames the mirror.

Inside the Kakinoki Antique Gallery

Blue and white
places, spaces, sources

Antiques

Akariya
4-8-1 Yoyogi,
Shibuya-ku, Tokyo
03 3465 5578

Antique John
1-6-33 Higashi,
Kunitachi-shi, Tokyo
0425 76 6330

Antique Market
Hanae Mori Bldg. B1,
3-6-1 Kita Aoyama,
Minato-ku, Tokyo
03 3400 3301

Antiques Hasebeya
1-5-24 Azabu Juban,
Minato-ku, Tokyo
03 3401 9998

Bo Peep
1230 Naganuma-cho,
Hachioji-shi, Tokyo
0426 35 1540

Gallery Hasebeya
3-11-3 Moto Azabu,
Minato-ku, Tokyo
03 3401 8840

Harumi Antiques
9-6-14 Akasaka,
Minato-ku, Tokyo
03 3403 1043

Karakusa
5-13-1 Minami Aoyama,
Minato-ku, Tokyo
03 3499 5858

Kawano Gallery
(antique kimono)
102 Flats Omotesando,
4-4-9 Jingumae,
Shibuya-ku, Tokyo
03 3470 3305
also at:
15 Okinohata,
Yanagawa-shi,
Fukuoka Prefecture
0944 73 0131

Kikori Antiques
Hanae Mori Bldg. B1,
3-6-1 Kita Aoyama,
Minato-ku, Tokyo
03 3407 9363

Kochian
4-323-1 Tomoda-machi,
Ome-shi, Tokyo
0428 22 0997

Kurofune
(John Adair)
7-7-4 Roppongi,
Minato-ku, Tokyo
03 3479 1552

Magatani
5-10-13 Toranomon,
Minato-ku, Tokyo
03 3433 6321

Makotoya
2-39-2 Wada,
Suginami-ku, Tokyo
03 3311 1609

Kathryn Milan
3-1-14 Nishi Azabu,
Minato-ku, Tokyo
03 3408 1532

Morita Antiques
5-12-2 Minami Aoyama,
Minato-ku, Tokyo
03 3407 4466

Nanshudo
5-18-9 Hiroo,
Shibuya-ku, Tokyo
03 3440 7408

Nishikawa Antiques
2-20-14 Azabu Juban,
Minato-ku, Tokyo
03 3456 1023

Okura Oriental Art
(Kenji Tsuchisawa)
3-3-14 Azabudai,
Minato-ku, Tokyo
03 3585 5309

Omoshiroya
(vintage kimono)
101, 1-11-21 Higashi-
machi, Kichijoji,
Musashino-shi, Tokyo
0422 22 8565

Setsu Getsu Ka
Christy Fuji Bldg. 2Fl.,
2-13-2 Azabu Juban,
Minato-ku, Tokyo
03 3452 7536

Galleries and Shops

Beniya
(folk crafts)
2-16-8 Shibuya,
Shibuya-ku, Tokyo
03 3400 8084

Bingoya
(folk crafts)
10-6 Wakamatsu-cho,
Shinjuku-ku, Tokyo
03 3202 8778

Blue & White
2-9-2 Azabu Juban,
Minato-ku, Tokyo
03 3451 0537

Fudoki
5-18-10 Minami Aoyama,
Minato-ku, Tokyo
03 3407 3383

Gallery Mayu
(Yu Kobayashi pots)
1-2-10 Nishikata,
Bunkyo-ku, Tokyo
03 3814 1330

Gallery Shun
Sun Palace Bldg. 1Fl.,
4-2-49 Minami Azabu,
Minato-ku, Tokyo
03 3444 7665

Hanada
(ceramics)
2-2-5 Kudan Minami,
Chiyoda-ku, Tokyo
03 3262 0669

**Japan Traditional
Craft Center**
Plaza 246 Bldg. 2Fl.,
3-1-1 Minami Aoyama,
Minato-ku, Tokyo
03 3403-2460

Kamawanu
(tenugui)
23-1 Sarugaku-cho,
Shibuya-ku, Tokyo
03 3780 0182

Mitsukoshi
(department store)
Ebisu Garden Place,
4-20-7 Ebisu,
Shibuya-ku, Tokyo
03 5423 1111

Noya
(tenugui)
5-12-3 Ginza,
Chuo-ku, Tokyo
03 3541 0975

Savoir Vivre
(ceramics)
Axis Bldg. 3Fl.,
5-17-1 Roppongi,
Minato-ku, Tokyo
03 3585 7365

Sei
(indigo textiles)
Hanae Mori Bldg. B1,
3-6-1 Kita Aoyama,
Minato-ku, Tokyo
03 3407 7541

Silk Lab
2-30-4 Numabukuro,
Nakano-ku, Tokyo
03 3389 4301

Takumi
(craft shop & gallery)
8-4-2 Ginza,
Chuo-ku, Tokyo
03 3571 2017

Toukyo
(gallery)
2-25-13 Nishi Azabu,
Minato-ku, Tokyo,
03 3797 4494

Tsukasa (wild flowers
arranged in antique or
unusual containers)
3-7-21 Ginza,
Chuo-ku, Tokyo
03 3535 6929
also at:
45 Mori Bldg. 1Fl.,
5-1-5 Toranomon,
Minato-ku, Tokyo
03 3431 6801

Uchida
(gallery)
2-8-6 Azabu Juban,
Minato-ku, Tokyo
03 3455 4595

**Yokohama Sogo
Japan Shop**
2-18-1 Takashima,
Nishi-ku, Yokohama-shi,
Kanagawa Prefecture
045 465 2111 ext. 5686

Yoshicho
(blue & white ceramics)
1-11-4 Nishi Azabu,
Minato-ku, Tokyo
03 3402 9480

Antiques Outside Tokyo

Chinpun Kanpun
Iizuka Atsushi,
2511-61 Isshiki,
Hayama-machi,
Miura-gun,
Kanagawa Prefecture
0468 75 0944

House of Antiques
(Yoshihiro Takishita)
2-15-3 Kajiwara,
Kamakura-shi,
Kanagawa Prefecture
0467 43 1441

Kakinoki
(Susumu Kakitani)
212-6 Kita Akitsu,
Tokorozawa-shi,
Saitama Prefecture,
0429 95 0626

Kura 50
(Sanae Imaeda)
Hanado 50, Takaya-cho,
Konan-shi,
Aichi Prefecture
0587 55-3314

**Nakamura
Chingireya-ten**
(antique textiles)
Furumonzen Agaru,
Yamatoji-dori,
Higashiyama-ku, Kyoto
075 561 4726

Noboriya
Kitamura, Yoshichiku
5223 Yamaguchi,
Tokorozawa-shi
0429 28 2666

Tora Antiques
(Erika Yamada)
1-4-8 Honcho,
Nagaoka-shi,
Niigata Prefecture
0258 39 0602

Galleries, Shops, and Craftsmen Outside Tokyo

Akitsuya
53 Kami Ichi no Machi,
Takayama,
Gifu Prefecture
0577 34 5053

Awagami
141 Kawa-higashi,
Yamakawa-cho, Oe-gun,
Tokushima Prefecture
0883 42 6120

Haruri Ginka
3-3 Saiwai-cho,
Kawagoe-shi,
Saitama Prefecture
0492 24 8689

Hyugaji Folk Crafts
1-16-5 Hiroshima-dori,
Miyazaki-shi,
Miyazaki Prefecture,
Kyushu
0985 22 8338

Kame no i Craft Shop
2633 Oaza Kawakami,
Yufuin-cho, Oita-gun,
Oita Prefecture
0977 853301

Kogensha
(folk crafts)
2-18 Zaimoku-cho,
Morioka-shi,
Iwate Prefecture
0196 22 2894

Kudaka Mingei
(folk crafts)
2-3-2 Makishi,
Naha-shi, Okinawa
098 861 6690

Maekawa, Hideki
(sculptor)
1159-18 Shimotomi,
Tokorozawa-shi,
Saitama Prefecture
0429 43 5741

Moyai Kogei
2-1-10 Sasuke,
Kamakura-shi,
Kanagawa Prefecture
0467 22 1822

**Nomoto, Kibo and
Keiko** (potter and
indigo artist)
Aoyagi, Seichoji,
Sakakitamura,
Higashi Chikuma-gun
Nagano Prefecture
0263 66 3768

Noto Nigyo Washi
Nigyo, Mitsui-machi,
Wajima-shi,
Ishikawa Prefecture
0768 26 1314

Omine, Jissei
(potter)
2653-1 Zakimi,
Yomitan-son,
Nakagami-gun,
Okinawa
0989 58 2828

Tefu Tefu
3 Asaichi-dori,
Kawai-cho,
Wajima-shi,
Ishikawa Prefecture
0768 22 6304

Yu Craft
10-7 Sawai-cho,
Kanazawa-shi,
Ishikawa Prefecture
0762 24 0015

Dyers, Weavers, and Others

Aizen Kobo
Nakasuji-dori,
Omiya Nishi-iru,
Kamigyo-ku, Kyoto
075 441 0355

Kosoen
8-200 Nagabuchi,
Ome-shi, Tokyo
0428 24 8121

Kudaka Mingei
2-3-2 Makishi,
Naha-shi,
Okinawa
098 861 6690

Makishi, Tamiko
1336 Aza Maeda,
Uresoe-shi,
Okinawa
098 877 0518

**Matsubara Senshoku
Kobo**
2-20-7 Matsushima,
Edogawa-ku, Tokyo
03 3651 3729

Takemura Sangyo
106 Kamimurakimi,
Hanyu-shi,
Saitama Prefecture
0485 65 2030

Tanaka, Kenji and Aiko
Kobo Ai
3332-1392 Kami-Sasao,
Kobuchisawa-cho,
Yamanashi Prefecture
0551 36 4361

**Watanabe
Somemono Ten**
Tatemachi
Hachiman-cho,
Gujo-gun,
Gifu Prefecture
0575 65 3959

**Yomitan-son Kyodo
Hanbai Center**
(craft co-op & restaurant)
2723-1 Aza Zakimi,
Yomitan-son, Okinawa
098 958 1020

32 craftsmen, including:

Inamine, Seikichi
(glassmaker)

Omine, Jissei
(potter)

**Shimabukuro,
Tsunehide**
(potter)

Yamada, Shinman
(potter)

Museums

**Arimatsu Narumi
Shibori Kaikan**
60-1 Hashi Higashi
Minami, Arimatsu-cho,
Midori-ku, Nagoya-shi,
Aichi Prefecture
052 621 0111

Kurita Museum
2-17-9 Nihonbashi,
Hama-cho,
Chuo-ku, Tokyo
03 3666 6246

**Izumo Folk Arts
Museum**
628 Chiimiya-cho,
Izumo-shi,
Shimane Prefecture
0853 22 6397

**Japan Folk Craft
Museum**
(Mingei-kan)
4-3-33 Komaba,
Meguro-ku, Tokyo
03 3467 4527

**Kurashiki Museum of
Folk Crafts**
1-4-11 Chuo,
Kurashiki-shi,
Okayama Prefecture
0864 22 1637

**Matsumoto Folk
Craft Museum**
1313-1 Shimokanai,
Satoyamabe,
Matsumoto-shi,
Nagano Prefecture
0263 33 1569

**Serizawa Keisuke
Museum**
5-10-5 Toro,
Shizuoka-shi,
Shizuoka Prefecture
0542 82 5522

Suntory Museum
Suntory Bldg. 11Fl.,
1-2-3 Moto Akasaka,
Minato-ku, Tokyo
03 3470 1073

Toguri Museum
1-11-3 Shoto,
Shibuya-ku, Tokyo
03 3465 0070

Toyama Museum
675 Shiroinuma,
Kawajima-machi,
Hiki-gun,
Saitama Prefecture
0492 97 0007

**Yuasa Hachiro
Museum**
International Christian
University,
3-10-2 Osawa,
Mitaka-shi, Tokyo
0422 33 3340

**Yufuin Kuso no Mori
Art Museum**
Torigoe, Yufuin-cho,
Oita-gun,
Oita Prefecture, Kyushu
0977 85 4007

Restaurants

Hiroo Kiraku
Sun Palace Bldg. 1Fl.,
4-2-49 Minami Azabu,
Minato-ku, Tokyo
03 3444 8971

Katsukichi Tonkatsu
Zen Suido Kaikan Bldg.
1-4-1 Hongo
Bunkyo-ku, Tokyo
03 3812 6268

Kisso
Axis Bldg. B1,
5-17-1 Roppongi,
Minato-ku, Tokyo
03 3582 4191

**Rêves de Vie
Centre Français des Arts**
2-12-1 Shiroganedai,
Minato-ku, Tokyo
03 3444 5711

Flea Markets

**First Sunday of the
month** Arai Yakushi
Temple (Arai Yakushiji-
mae Station on the
Seibu Shinjuku Line)

**First and fourth
Sundays** Togo Shrine
(Harajuku Station on
the Yamanote Line or
Meiji-Jingumae Station
on the Chiyoda Line)

Second Sunday Nogi
Shrine (Nogizaka
Station on the Chiyoda
Line); Kumagawa
Shrine (Fussa City)

Third Sunday
Hanazono Shrine
(Shinjuku San-chome
Station on the
Marunouchi Line)

Third Sunday
Takahata Fudo,
Hino City,
Tokyo

**Third Thursday and
Friday of each month**
Roi Building (Roppongi
Station on the Hibiya
Line)

**Twenty-first of each
month, rain or shine**
Toji Temple, Kyoto

**Twenty-fifth of each
month, rain or shine**
Kitano Tenjin Shrine,
Kyoto

**Twenty-eighth of each
month** Narita Fudo
Shrine (Kawagoe,
Saitama Prefecture, on
the Tobu Line)

**December 15, 16 and
January 15, 16**
Boro Ichi (Setagaya
Station on the
Setagaya Line)
Tokyo

**March, May,
June, September,
December**
Heiwajima Antiques Fair
(Ryutsu Center Station
on the Tokyo Monorail
from Hamamatsucho
Station)

Blue and white vocabulary

Aizome Indigo dyeing

Arita Porcelains, blue and white and otherwise, made in Arita, Kyushu

Bangasa Japanese paper umbrella

Bashofu Banana-fiber cloth

Daikon White radish

Furoshiki Square carrying cloth

Futon Sleeping quilt

Genkan Entrance

Hibachi Brazier for warming the hands

Imari Porcelains, originally blue and white, named for the port in Kyushu from which they were shipped

Irori Sunken open hearth

Jimbei Two-piece cotton suit

Karakusa Arabesque

Kasuri Patterned blue and white cloth

Katazome Stencil dyeing

Kotatsu Covered foot-warming table

Maneki neko Figurine of a cat with raised paw (thought to invite prosperity)

Momen Cotton

Monpe Baggy cotton work pants, usually *kasuri* and usually for women

Noren Divided doorway curtain

Noshi Folded paper (originally abalone) used to decorate a gift

Obi Sash for kimono

Onigiri Rice ball

Sakiori Ragweave

Sashiko Stitchery designs and reinforcements on cloth, usually indigo

Shibori Resist dyeing by tying, binding, sewing, or folding cloth to achieve designs

Shimenawa Sacred New Year's decoration of rice straw and paper

Shishi Temple dog or lion

Soba choko Cup used for dipping sauce for buckwheat noodles

Sometsuke Blue and white underglaze porcelain; design technique used to achieve such porcelain

Tansu Chest with drawers

Tenugui Long cotton hand towel with stenciled designs

Tsutsugaki Freehand design achieved by applying paste resist with a tube applicator before a textile is dyed

Uzumaki Spiral motif

Washi Japanese handmade paper

Yogi, yogu Padded kimono-shaped bedding

Yukata Kimono-shaped light cotton robe for after the bath and summer wear

Zabuton Floor cushion